IN THE NEXT THREE SECONDS

Written by Rowland Morgan

Illustrated by Rod and Kira Josey

HAMLYN

Editor: Beryl Creek
Art Director: Anne Sharples
Production Controller: Christine Campbell

Rod and Kira Josey are represented by Garden Studios, London

First published in 1997 by Hamlyn Children's Books,
an imprint of Reed Books, Children's Publishing Limited, Michelin House, 81 Fulham Road,
London SW3 6RB, Auckland and Melbourne.

ISBN 0 600 58937 4

Printed in Spain.

CONTENTS

INTRODUCTION......

Somebody's always measuring something, because there's so much going on.
The first counting was probably done by caterers for imperial banquets in ancient China. If they didn't plan enough food for the emperor's guests, he'd see their heads were chopped off. They planned ahead by counting and measuring, using beads on strings in a frame, a tool called an abacus.

Now people use a whole toolchest of equipment for measuring: slide-rules, stopwatches, clocks, timers, calculators, gauges, scales, balances, meters, monitors, probes, and of course, computers. Computers have compiled enormous hoards of information about everything under the sun (and plenty about the sun as well).

Practically every move we make is noted somewhere by an electronic brain: from issuing text books at school to buying sweets at the corner shop. People feed information into computers about almost everything, from the movements of microbes to the deeds of dinosaurs. The facts in this book are worked out from this great new form of wealth called information. It's a kind of wealth that does not harm the environment, does not pollute, and is interesting without end – as we hope this book will show!

Now, in the next three minutes, how much of it will you read?

HOW TO MAKE YOUR OWN PREDICTIONS

First, choose a fact in the past that you find interesting. Lots of interesting statistics are quoted on the TV, in the newspapers or in schoolbooks, supplying you with measures of the past. Then find some conclusions you can draw by working out how this fact can be turned into an average measurement of some kind.
For example: bottled water factories told a sales survey conducted by a marketing firm (Euromonitor plc) that they sold 7.5 litres of mineral water per Briton in a recent year (in Italy it was 101, by the way).
How much mineral water will Britons use in the next three days?

First, multiply the number of Britons by the litres of packaged water they use:

58,000,000 x 7.5 = 435 million

Then divide that total by the number of days in a year:

435,000,000 ÷ 365 = 1,191,780 litres a day

To find three days, multiply by three:

1,191,780 x 3 = 3,575,342 litres

There is your prediction: In The Next Three Days, Britons will glug nearly 3.6 million litres of mineral water. Now try expressing that rather long number in a way that is easier to imagine.

For example: a typical bath-tub holds 150 litres. So work out the number of bath-tubs of mineral water Britons will use in the next three days thus:

3,575,342 ÷ 150 = 23,835 bath-tubfuls

Perhaps it is still hard to imagine so many bathtubs of water, so how about another conversion? A juggernaut road-tanker carries approximately 32,000 litres, so work out your prediction in road-tankers, as follows:

3,575,342 ÷ 32,000 = 111 articulated road-tankers

If you still think it is hard to picture so many tankers, why not make a queue of them? An articulated road-tanker is 15 metres long. Allow half a metre parking distance each end, i.e. 16 metres, and make the following calculation:

111 x 16 = 1,776m or 1.78 km

So your prediction becomes: In the next three days, Britons will drink enough mineral water to fill a queue of juggernaut lorries nearly two kilometres long!

Here are some useful figures for making conversions:

Bathtub .... 150 litres
Juggernaut lorry .... 25 tonnes (15 metres long)
Juggernaut tanker .... 32,000 litres
Supertanker .... 100,000 tonnes
Olympic swimming pool .... 2.27 million litres
Tarbela Dam (world's biggest) .... weighs 242 million tonnes
Airliner fuel consumption .... 50 litres per mile
Wembley Stadium (if filled) .... 1 million cubic metres
Tennis court .... 264 sq metres
Soccer field .... 2.7 acres
Toaster .... 800 watts

IN THE NEXT THREE SECONDS...

the Sun.....

Your heart will beat nearly 3 times

The Planet Earth will orbit 91 KILOMETRES round

Japanese eaters will throw 'away' 2 pairs of CHOPSTICKS made from felled Malaysian Rainforests

The human population will increase by NINE

Motor Vehicles will use 3 road tankers of petrol

Americans will buy 56 air-conditioning units

RUSSIANS WILL MAIL MORE THAN 4,000 LETTERS OR PARCELS

MAGICAL MYSTERY TOUR

Enough tourists to FILL a bus will arrive

A Sei Whale could dive 53 Metres at the speed of a Naval Submarine

A CRUISING Boeing 757 airliner will burn three cupfuls of KEROSENE in the arid upper atmosphere

SOME~WHERE

LOGGERS will cut down 799 trees

93 trees will be cut down to make the liners for disposable nappies

CHINESE PEOPLE WILL BUY 3 NEW COLOUR T.V.S

A TGV Express train in FRANCE will travel the length of eight tennis courts

TGV

Britons will CONSUME a stack of 500gm tins of baked beans four times as high as St.Paul's Cathedral

6

Italians will DRINK a stack of cases of mineral water as HIGH as the Statue of Liberty

AMERICANS will eat 6,000 eggs

95 AIRLINERS WILL TAKE OFF

106 children around the world will receive a vaccine jab...

3 teddy bears will be given

A flying midge (Genus Forcipomyia) will beat its wings 3,100 times

Irish people will drink 200 potfuls of tea

Four new MOTOR vehicles will be driven out of FACTORIES

Americans will buy eight dishwashers

A Sprinting Cheetah will cover three-quarters... the length of a soccer field

18 years' worth of TELEVISION will be watched by people round the world

The place where you are now on Earth... will revolve 1.4 kilometres eastwards

Italians will kill 10 song birds for bite-size morsels

Americans will throw 'away' 3,000 aluminium drink cans

US Cola 50¢

A barefoot Fijian could climb 1.8 metres up a Coconut Tree

The holder of the world land speed record could pass 212 parked cars

Britons will eat 3,600 potatoes

RODENTS WILL EAT ENOUGH TO FEED 19 STARVING PEOPLE

Eleven tourists will Arrivé in France

saskatchewan farmers will produce 90 tonnes of wheat, enough for **200,000** loaves

An animated cartoon will use 4,320 pictures

IN THE NEXT THREE MINUTES...

People on Earth will eat the weight of 100 Great Blue Whales (NB 13,000 tonnes of food)

A wild fox will be trapped & skinned by Canadian Furriers for rich people's wardrobes

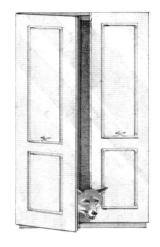

British doctors will write 750 prescriptions for Asthma

A baby will be born to an unmarried mother in Britain

The green man will SHINE at the pelican crossing seven times

Drivers will travel far enough on Western European motorways to go round the world 45 times

People on Earth will take six railcars of aspirins

Germans will buy a stack of personal stereos two metres HIGH

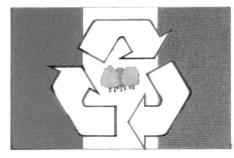

French people will save a copse of 600 trees by recycling paper

You will secrete 2 millilitres of saliva

French ladies will buy a pick-up of toilet soap (NB 1.5 tonnes)

World farm~ers will spread 100 pick-up loads of compound chemical fertilizers (NB 1,400 tonnes)

Chinese builders will pour six semi-trailer truck loads of concrete for the 20-year Three Gorges dam project on the Yangtse River

Americans will buy a stack of new major electrical appliances as tall as one of the world's tallest buildings, the Sears Tower, Chicago

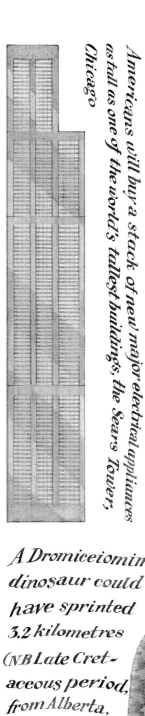

Enough razors will be junked by West European shavers to follow the white line along the

Calais to Geneva Road (780km)

Fishermen will kill more than 25 wild porpoises or dolphins

The Super Nintendo console will recognise 10,588 different signals from the official control pad

A poacher will kill a wild Elephant in central Africa

People will buy 176 mobile phones

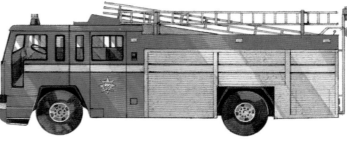

British fire brigades will put out 2.4 fires

A Dromiceiomimus dinosaur could have sprinted 3.2 kilometres (NB Late Cretaceous period, from Alberta, Canada)

British dairy cows will give 84 pails of cream (NB 10-LITRE pail)

Euro-shops will take delivery of enough throw-away aerosol cans to fill more than five kilometres of shelving

Children in 1.5 British families will see their parents divorce

Americans will eat four-and-a-half head of cattle as fast-food take-out hamburgers

Germans will buy a stack of 119 colour TVs over twice as high as the walls of the Kremlin Palace in MOSCOW

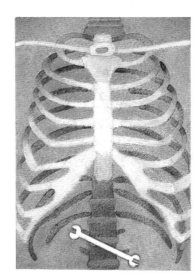

British public service surgeons will perform 24 free-of-charge operations

Seventeen species of life will disappear from the tropical rainforests

IN THE NEXT THREE HOURS...

Certain useful types of bamboo will grow 23cms in the...

MENU -
Americans will eat 600,000 lobsters

Americans will buy 4,500 pairs of jeans

Sewage the weight of 80 Paris Arc de Triomphes will be pumped into the harbour of Boston, U.S.A.

Meteosat, the weather satellite, will take a complete picture of the clouds over Europe, Africa and the Atlantic Ocean six times

A tonne of the planet's living coral will be broken off reefs for sale in souvenir shops

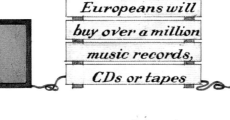

Europeans will buy over a million music records, CDs or tapes

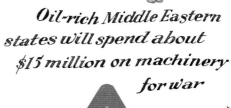

Oil-rich Middle Eastern states will spend about $15 million on machinery for war

A butterfly will transform from a pupa into a beautiful fluttering adult

Children will lose 11 hairs from their head which will be replaced (old folks lose 15 permanently)

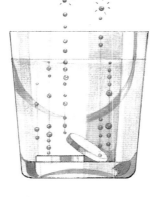

Americans will spend over $1 million on remedies for indigestion

Over 3,000 wild animals will be killed on Europe's roads

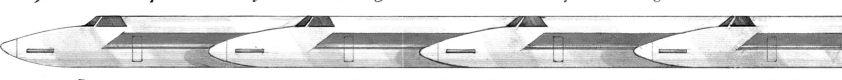

Four Bullet-Trains of people will be added to crowded Japan's population

Americans will use paper that requires 375,000 trees to make

Over 500 baby rabbits will be adopted as family pets

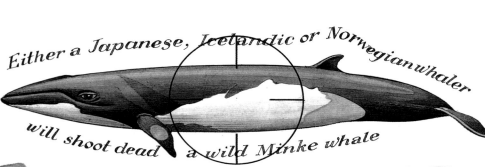

Either a Japanese, Icelandic or Norwegian whaler will shoot dead a wild Minke whale

Five aeroplanes will pass over the British Isles carrying radioactive materials

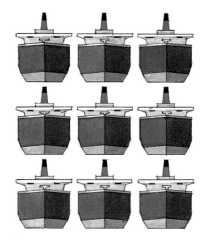

It's for you-hoo!

French people will spend $2 million on perfume

American smokers will THROW away a (horizontally-laid) stack of 350,000 cigarette lighters as high as Oregon's Mount Hood volcano

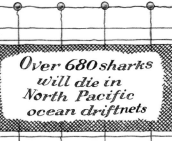

Over 680 sharks will die in North Pacific ocean driftnets

Germans will buy 20 stacks of dishwashers as high as the world's tallest totem pole at Alert Bay, BC, Canada

Nine OIL tankers will dock in British ports

Hardwood for 1,920 doors will be imported to Britain from tropical countries

Americans will buy a STACK of telephones four times as high as Toronto's CN communications tower

Italians will buy enough pairs of shoes to give everybody in Venice five pairs each

Americans will throw away 160 kilometres of plastic pens

BRITISH CATS & DOGS WILL BE FED ENOUGH PET FOOD TO FILL 1.2 MILLION TINS

In The Next Three Days...

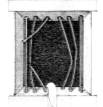

Britons will FLUSH away enough toilet paper to stretch to the MOON... and back

Over **1,000,000** new bicycles will be wheeled out of factories

Enough garbage to load two WORLD FLEETS of super-tankers will be dumped

Enough Aluminium will be thrown away

DOCTORS NOTE:

Your cold virus will multiply itself 10,000 million times before causing your first sneeze.

Four British children under three will have to be treated for a dogbite .....

A tonne of wood in a forest will release a tonne of oxygen O_2

A blue shark in a hurry could travel 2,500 kilometres or..... from Africa .... to India

A koala bear might well sleep for sixty-six hours

DO NOT DISTURB

A rickshaw puller in Calcutta, India will earn $3

JOURNEY INTO SPACE

West Europeans will smoke 460 pick-up trucks of cured tobacco

North Americans will truck enough sand and gravel to make concrete for more than 1,200 New York World Trade Centers

Enough writing will move on the computer Internet to make a stack of **THICK** paperback books reaching into outer space (60 kilometres)

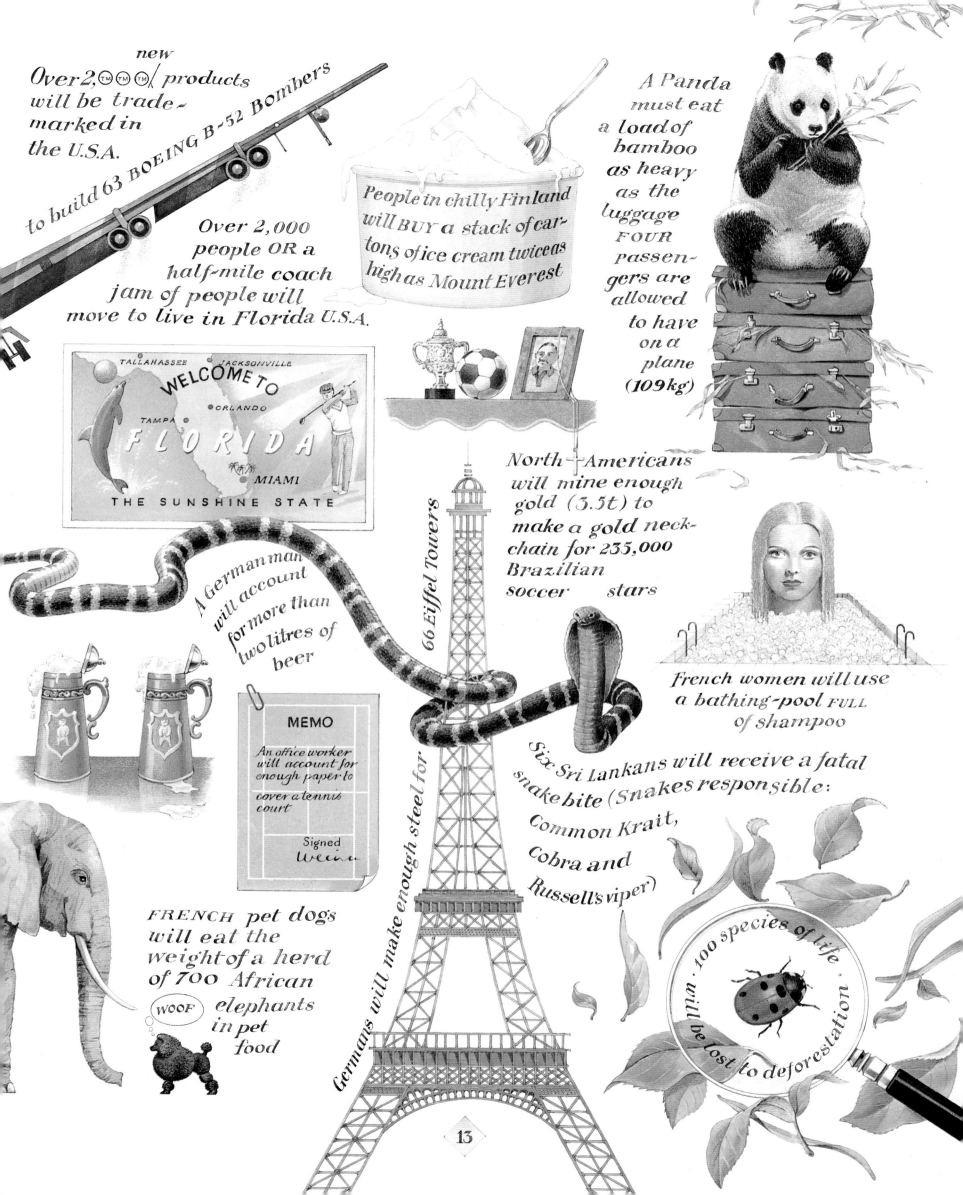

Over 2,000 (TM)(TM)(TM) new products will be trade-marked in the U.S.A.

to build 63 BOEING B-52 Bombers

Over 2,000 people OR a half-mile coach jam of people will move to live in Florida U.S.A.

WELCOME TO
TALLAHASSEE · JACKSONVILLE
· ORLANDO
TAMPA
MIAMI
FLORIDA
THE SUNSHINE STATE

People in chilly Finland will BUY a stack of cartons of ice cream twice as high as Mount Everest

A Panda must eat a load of bamboo as heavy as the luggage FOUR passengers are allowed to have on a plane (109 kg)

North-Americans will mine enough gold (3.5 t) to make a gold neck-chain for 235,000 Brazilian soccer stars

A German man will account for more than two litres of beer

66 Eiffel Towers

MEMO
An office worker will account for enough paper to cover a tennis court
Signed
Weina

French women will use a bathing-pool FULL of shampoo

Six Sri Lankans will receive a fatal snake bite (Snakes responsible: Common Krait, Cobra and Russell's viper)

FRENCH pet dogs will eat the weight of a herd of 700 African elephants in pet food

WOOF

Germans will make enough steel for

100 species of life will be lost to deforestation

13

About 250 million Motor vehicles...

In The Next Three Nights...

More than 80 UFO sightings will be reported round the WORLD

OVER $15 MILLION DOLLARS WILL BE SPENT ON ADVERTISING FUEL-WASTING CARS TO AMERICANS

$15

Somalians will give their nanny goats about 45 million dawn milkings

150 jumbo-jet loads of people will starve to death

Distribution staff of the YOMIURI SHIMBUN will send 26 million copies of the newspaper across Japan

Three MILLION babies will be conceived...

MEXICO

450,000 tourists will spend a night in Mexico

The American Post Office will rush more than 740 million pieces of first class mail. ...nearly half the world total

12,000 Americans will brush their teeth with a newly-purchased

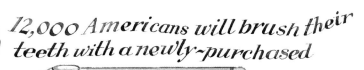

ELECTRIC TOOTHBRUSH

850 Australians will fly to SETTLE in crowded Britain..

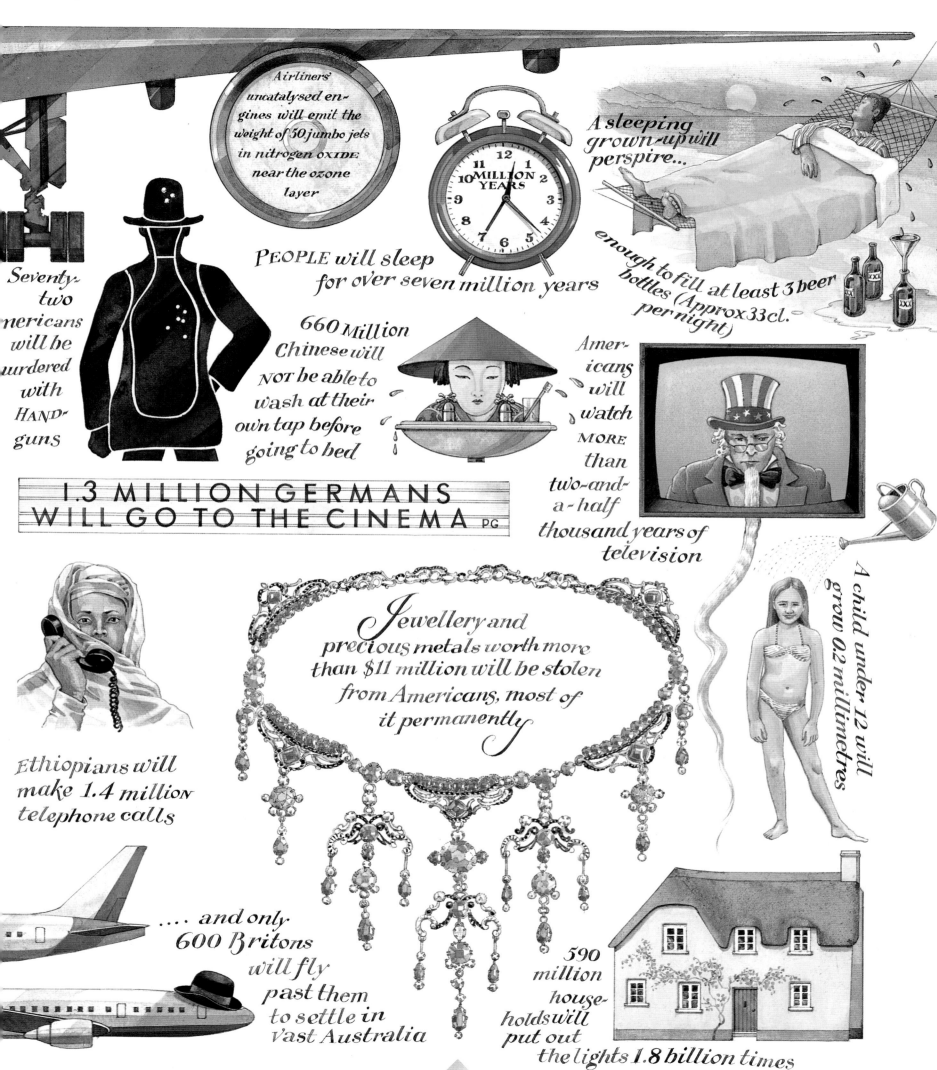

Airliners' uncatalysed engines will emit the weight of 50 jumbo jets in nitrogen OXIDE near the ozone layer

MILLION YEARS

PEOPLE will sleep for over seven million years

A sleeping grown-up will perspire...

enough to fill at least 3 beer bottles (Approx 33 cl. per night)

Seventy-two Americans will be murdered with HAND-guns

660 Million Chinese will NOT be able to wash at their own tap before going to bed

Americans will watch MORE than two-and-a-half thousand years of television

1.3 MILLION GERMANS WILL GO TO THE CINEMA PG

Ethiopians will make 1.4 million telephone calls

Jewellery and precious metals worth more than $11 million will be stolen from Americans, most of it permanently

A child under 12 will grow 0.2 millimetres

.... and only 600 Britons will fly past them to settle in vast Australia

590 million households will put out the lights 1.8 billion times

15

345 POP- songs will be released as singles in the UK

IN THE NEXT THREE WEEKS...

An American child could view over 1,000 acts of violence on television

500 square kms of solar furnaces in the Sahara Desert working at 10% efficiency could supply all the world's electricity

Americans will eat 80 pizzas as BIG as the White House presidential estate

More than 12,000 West European women will be caught shoplifting

The leaning tower of PISA will move another 0.073 millimetres off vertical

France will spend the value of 725 Mona Lisas subsi-dising Art & Culture

141 pedigree Rottweilers will be registered by British dog fanciers

GRRR!

Twenty cyclists will be killed in Shanghai traffic

Diplomats of Her Majesty the Qu_ a stack of SIX-packs of champag_

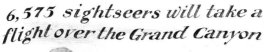

FIVE satellite launching rockets will tear a hole in the Earth's protec-tive ozone layer

6,575 sightseers will take a flight over the Grand Canyon

132,000 people will visit the Tower of London

The cars of 90,000 world drivers will go permanently

134 Doctors will emi-grate to Israel

£170 000

British TAX payers will spend £170,000 on solar power research (and £7.5 million on nuclear power research)

MISS-ING

MDJ 20

Three people will be KILLED or wounded in a fight in Los Angeles County, home of Holly-wood

The young herb Puya Raimondii will move one-thirteen-hundredth nearer the flowering of its only panicle in at least eighty years' time

HOLLYWOOD

China's SMOKE stacks will give off nine super-tanker loads of acid rain-making Sulphur Dioxide

SO_2

ll spend enough on parties to buy r times higher than the Taj Mahal

In The Next Three Months...

Five hundred new CD-ROMs will be published for multimedia computers

Europeans will junk a stack of cans three times (102,000 kms) higher than a (geostationary) weather satellite

American offices will use 194 billion pieces of paper, enough to make 4,000 STACKS higher than Mount Kanchenjunga (8,598m)

(N.B 35,000 kilometres high)

4 million TV video-game machines will be sold world-wide

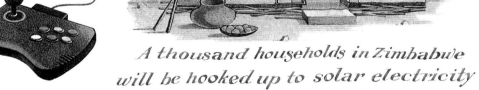

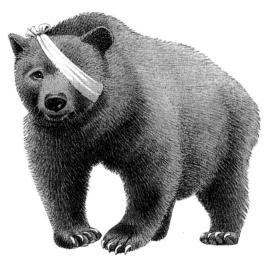

Seventy endangered Florida black bears will be lethally hit by road traffic

A thousand households in Zimbabwe will be hooked up to solar electricity

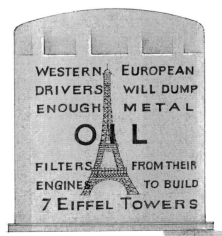

WESTERN EUROPEAN DRIVERS WILL DUMP ENOUGH METAL OIL FILTERS FROM THEIR ENGINES TO BUILD 7 EIFFEL TOWERS

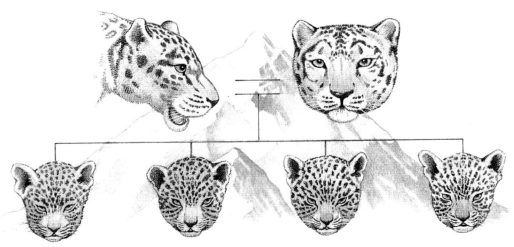

At least one extra family of baby snow leopards will be born in new game parks established around Mt. Everest in Nepal

Over 12 million personal computers will be sold world-wide ... one for each European Union child aged 5~15

An uncatalysed car using leaded fuel and doing average mileage will emit LEAD weighing more than two soft-drink cans (69 grams)

45 million households ~ twice the number in Britain ~ will be added to the world television audience

Countries will sign 43 NEW International environmental treaties

The U.S.A. and Russia will dismantle 1,290 nuclear BOMBS (NB or warheads)

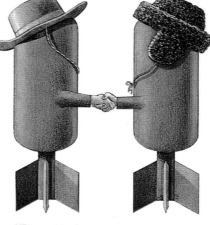

Eighty million more people will be added to those living in world cities

500 cinema feature films will be produced ... more than a solid month of round-the-clock screening time

Enough soybeans will be grown to outweigh seven Great Pyramids of Cheops

Over 120,000 Amazon parrots will be carried overseas and sold as pets

The average American's lifestyle will require the equivalent of 5,400 buckets of coal, the average Nigerian's, 100 (NB 27 tonnes, 0.5 tonne)

As part of a consumer society, your lifestyle will account for about five hot-air balloons of climate-changing carbon dioxide being emitted

An England size area of Siberian pine-forest will be clear-cut

NB 130,000 sq.km

Enough cars will be added to the world fleet to clog

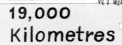

19,000 Kilometres

of six-lane highway

100,000 new mid-sized Buick cars will be SOLD for the first time to Chinese communists

One rat could have

2 0, 0 0 0, 0 0 0

DESCENDANTS

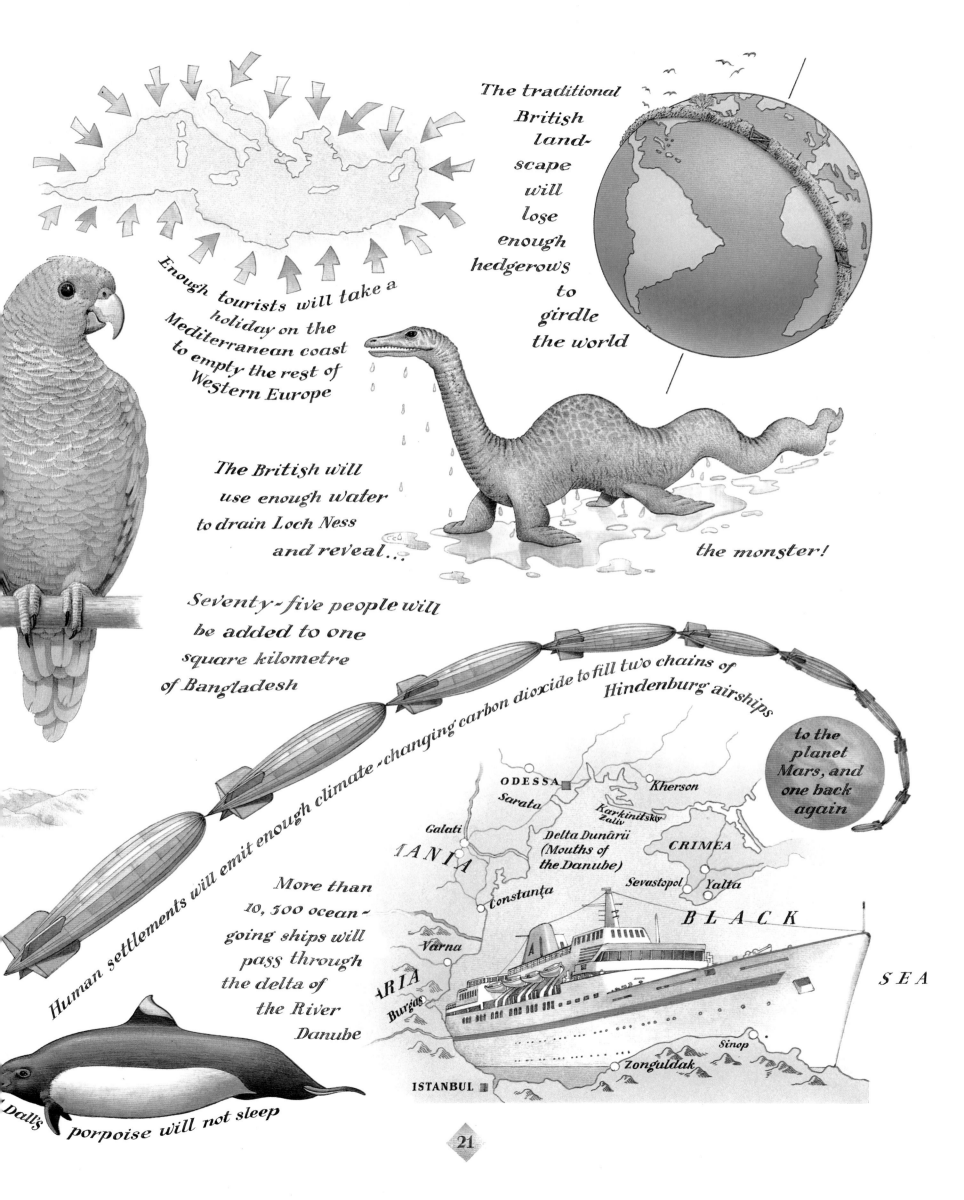

Enough tourists will take a holiday on the Mediterranean coast to empty the rest of Western Europe

The traditional British landscape will lose enough hedgerows to girdle the world

The British will use enough water to drain Loch Ness and reveal... the monster!

Seventy-five people will be added to one square kilometre of Bangladesh

Human settlements will emit enough climate-changing carbon dioxide to fill two chains of Hindenburg airships to the planet Mars, and one back again

More than 10,500 ocean-going ships will pass through the delta of the River Danube

Dall's porpoise will not sleep

ODESSA
Sarata
Kherson
Karkinitskiy Zaliv
Galati
Delta Dunării (Mouths of the Danube)
CRIMEA
ʻANIA
Constanța
Sevastopol
Yalta
Varna
BLACK
ʻARIA
Burgos
SEA
Zonguldak
Sinop
ISTANBUL

More people will probably be ADDED to the world population than existed on Earth when the Queen of England was seven (NB that was 1933)

More than three Million American women will have their nose changed…

1. $4,500
2. $7,000
3. $6,750
4. $5,800
5. $3,000
10 $5,500
11 $8,250
12

…by surgery

Pesticides the weight of 113 Exxon Valdez supertankers will be spread over Europe (NB 24 m tonnes)

Casualty nurses will attend to enough English accident and emergency victims to populate the whole of Western Europe

Pairs of skylarks, endangered in built-up countries, will raise fledglings 30 million times in the grasslands of high-plateau Turkey

HELP!

Winners of Britain's National Lottery...

Pairs of very rare white-tailed eagles will try to nest 240 times in the British Isles

...will take HOME enough money to give every child in the country an income of £119 a year

Firefighters will rescue nearly one million Londoners locked out of their homes and offices ~ or locked in!

On past form, Europe could lose an area of permanent meadows and pastures more than twice the size of Great Britain (NB 537, 355 sq. km 1960~90)

100 million European women will be wedded

3,000 Britons will have their portrait painted by Royal Society artists

IN THE NEXT THREE CENTURIES...

Countless new varieties of

| FLOWERS, | VEGETABLES, | FRUIT AND | DOMESTIC | ANIMALS |

will be bred for human and animal use

Human settlements on the planet MARS will house more than 50,000 pioneers, with at least 9,000 children *

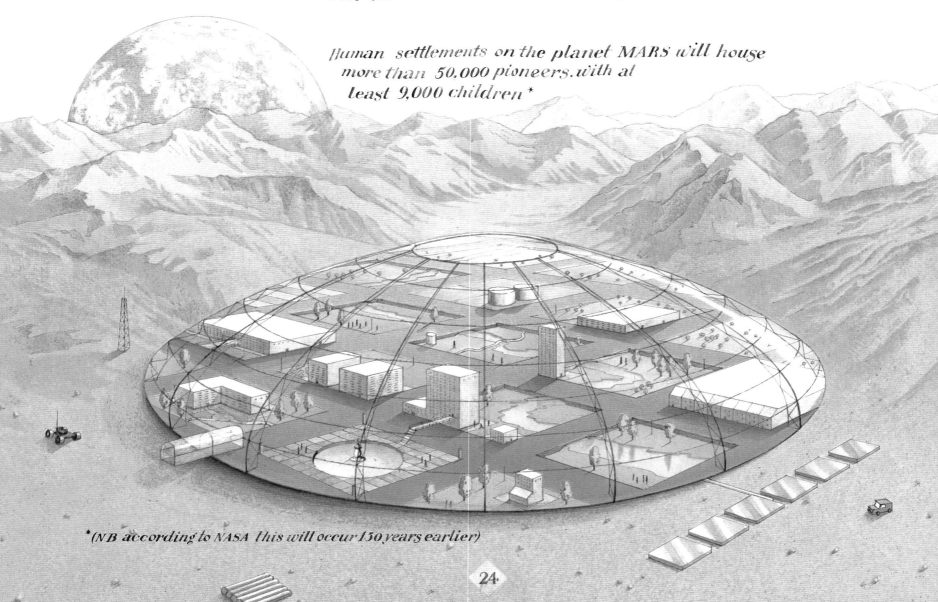

*(NB according to NASA this will occur 150 years earlier)

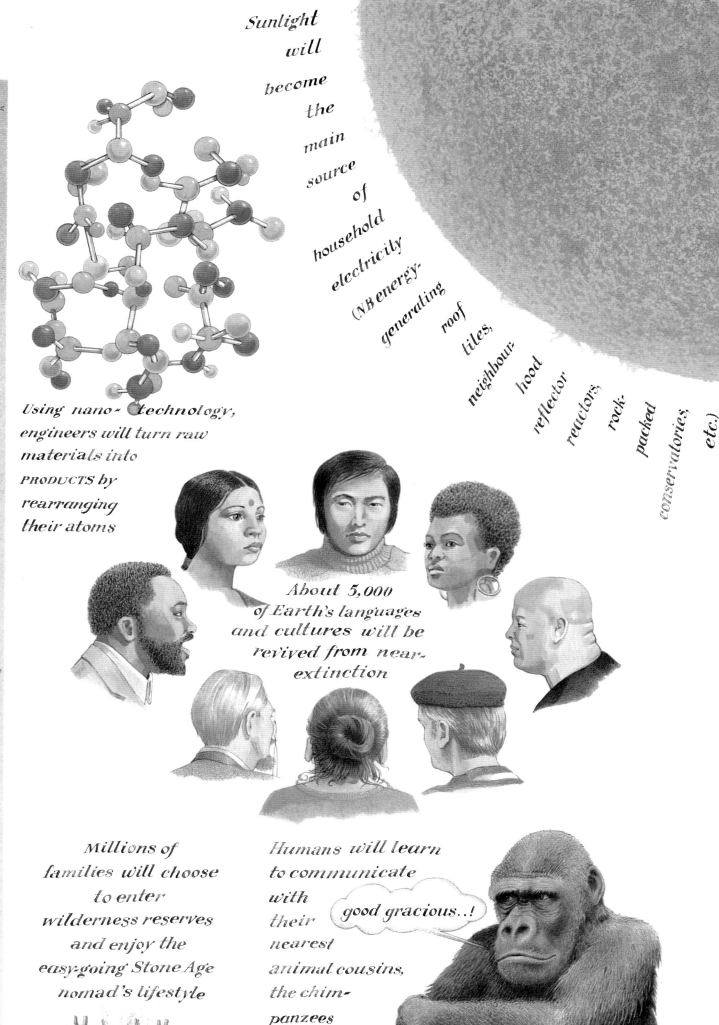

Using nano-technology, engineers will turn raw materials into PRODUCTS by rearranging their atoms

Sunlight will become the main source of household electricity (NB energy-generating roof tiles, neighbour-hood reflector reactors, rock-packed conservatories, etc.)

About 5,000 of Earth's languages and cultures will be revived from near-extinction

Millions of families will choose to enter wilderness reserves and enjoy the easy-going Stone Age nomad's lifestyle

Humans will learn to communicate with their nearest animal cousins, the chimpanzees baboons and gorillas

good gracious..!

25

IN THE NEXT THREE THOUSAND YEARS...

A precious antique 1997 clock losing half a second per day will only be six days behind

A hot-air balloon averaging 40KPH will have circled the planet 26,726 times

Due to a world-wide ban on poaching, forests should be home to at least 32 million MORE wild Lynx (NB based on 10,775 trapped skins sold a year)

On present trends, the icy North... and South poles will have melted

At current rates of global warming, the sea level will have risen between five and eighteen metres, submerging most human settlements

27

IN THE NEXT
THREE MILLION YEARS...

The space probe
VOYAGER 2
will be leaving
our galaxy,
the Milky Way

ACKNOWLEDGEMENTS

All predictions are based on published official, trade or reference sources. Principal sources for statistics calculated for use in this book: Parliamentary Debates, The Official Report (Hansard); Euromonitor plc; Panos Institute; Demos; BP plc; Worldwatch Institute; MORI; Driver & Vehicle Licensing Agency; US Motor Vehicle Manuf. Assoc.; United Nations; US Environmental Protection Agency; BBC News & Current Affairs; Organisation for Economic Co-operation & Development (OECD); New Scientist; WARMER Bulletin; Whitakers Almanack; Hutchinson Encyclopedia; The Cambridge Encyclopedia; The Guinness Book of Records; Eurostat, Luxembourg; Statistical Abstract of the US; Information Please Environmental Almanac; US Office of Management & Budget; Quid, Paris; British Airways plc; The Pink Book, HMSO; Office of Population, Census & Surveys (OPCS); Canada Yearbook; Hutchinson Dictionary of Science; The Information Please Almanac; Planet Gauge, The Real Facts Of Life; Planet Gauge 1993.

THE AUTHOR thanks especially the staff of Richmond-Upon-Thames Reference Library.

INDEX